Jet, the rabbit, has a hutch
next to the shed. He has no
grass in it and he is hungry.

1

He bangs the door of his hutch and it opens. Jet jumps out and goes to look for some fresh grass.

2

Jelly and Bean see the empty hutch. Oh no! Where is Jet? The cats rush off to look for him.

Jelly looks in the hut. Jet is not there. Bean looks in the shed. Jet is not there.

Jelly looks in the mud. Jet is
not there. Bean looks in the
bushes. Jet is not there.

Then the cats see Jet in the ditch. He is eating the long grass. They rush to the ditch to catch him.

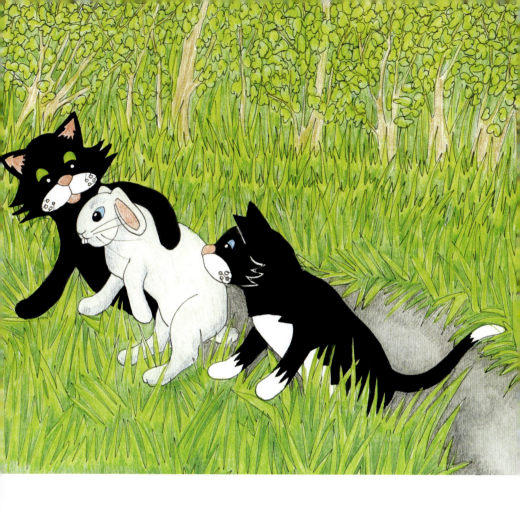

Jet has eaten so much grass he cannot run away. The cats have to help him back to his hutch.

They put some fresh grass in
the hutch for him and he falls
asleep eating it.